Adventures in the Holy Land

A Look at Israel

Jeffrey D. Johnson

Wipf & Stock
PUBLISHERS
Eugene, Oregon

Wipf and Stock Publishers
199 W 8th Ave, Suite 3
Eugene, OR 97401

Adventures in the Holy Land
A Look at Israel
By Johnson, Jeffrey D.

ISBN 13: 978-1-55635-083-2
ISBN 10: 1-55635-083-X
Publication date 11/30/2006

About Israel Today Ministries

Three-fold Purpose:

- Teach the Church about Israel
- Teach Israel about their Messiah
- Help feed those in need (Romans 15:27; Genesis 12:1-3)

To receive Dr. Johnson's "teaching letters," or, if you would like to send a gift to Israel Today Ministries, or if you would like Dr. Johnson to speak at your church event, school, or small group, contact:

Israel Today Ministries
P.O. Box 150288
Arlington, TX 76015
Phone/Fax 817.468.4441
E mail: Galileeman@juno.com

This is Yossef (Joseph) and Abigail. Your monthly donations help feed little ones like these.

"Inasmuch as ye have done it unto one of the least of these my brethren, ye have done it unto me" –Jesus, Matthew 25:40

About Dr. Jeffrey D. Johnson

- Three decades in ministry
- Founder/Director of Israel Today Ministries
- Director of tours to the Middle East
- Senior pastor in Ohio, Massachusetts and California
- Almost 7 years directorship with International Ministries to Israel (formerly, The American Association for Jewish Evangelism, where the famed Hyman Appelman was the first president)
- Conference speaker
- Bible expositor
- Guest lecturer
- Author

Born and raised in the Midwest, Dr. Johnson took his B.D. from Massillon Baptist College, his MA from Moody Bible Institute, and his Th.M. and Th.D. from Christian Bible College. His passion for Israel, the Jewish roots of Christianity and Bible prophecy, is well known. His teaching will stir your heart to follow the Lord and to love and *"pray for the peace of Jerusalem"* (Psalm 122:6).

As an "Itinerant Bible Teacher," Dr. Johnson will travel anywhere to proclaim God's redeeming Grace through our Lord and Savior Jesus the Messiah, *"to the Jew first, and also to the Greek"* (Romans 1:16).

His call is to *"Teach the Church about Israel; Teach Israel about their Messiah; and to feed those in need"* (Genesis 12:3; Romans 15:27).

Dr. Jeff and his wife, Louise, have purposed to serve the Lord trusting God to provide the funds and resources for their livelihood.

Israel Today Ministries, founded by Dr. Johnson, is a faith ministry, supported by "love offerings" from those desiring to bless Israel. Dr. Jeff and Louise have been commissioned and sent out by their home church.

Comments from Christian Leaders

I am pleased to recommend him to churches as an able expositor of the Word of God.

– *the late* **John Walvoord**, Chancellor,
Dallas Theological Seminary

A Bible Expositor with special insights on the origin, nature and destiny of God's chosen people, Israel.

– **John C. Whitcomb**, Bible Scholar, Author, Professor

A careful expositor of Scripture.

– **Homer Kent**, President Emeritus,
Grace College and Seminary

A practitioner of all that he preaches.

– **Paige Patterson**, former President of the
Southern Baptist Convention, President,
Southeastern Baptist Theological Seminary

He has a wonderful grasp of Jewish history and liturgy.

– **Edgar C. James**, Professor, Moody Bible Institute

He is a person who has been uniquely prepared by God to preach and teach about God's special people. Any one who hears him will come away with a great love for the people of Abraham.

–**Dick Dahlquist**, Chair, Pastoral Studies, Acting Dean,
Grace College of Graduate Studies

He has a gifted teaching ministry which encompasses Biblical prophecy and insights into modern-day Judaism.

–the late **Paul Tassell**, Bible Scholar, Author,
former National Representative of the G.A.R.B.C.

He has a great ministry.

– **LaVerne Butler**, former President of Mid-Continent Baptist College, Scholar, Conference Speaker, President, Pulpit Aflame

Your heart will be thrilled as he ministers the prophetic Scriptures.

– the late **Alden A. Gannett**, President Emeritus of Southeastern Bible College, Bible Scholar, Author, Conference Speaker, President, Gannett Ministries

He loves the people and nation of Israel. He has given himself to a thorough study of God's ancient people and of the prophetic.

– **Ivan H. French**, Pastor Emeritus, Pleasant View Bible Church, former Professor, Grace College and Seminary

Table of Contents

Chapter 1
Is God Through with the Jew?

Nearly four thousand years ago God chose a seventy-five year-old man from Mesopotamia and made a covenant with him. When God made this covenant with Abraham (Genesis 12:1-3) He began to communicate through a single "chosen" people. Through Abraham came the promised child Isaac, then Jacob, the twelve patriarchs through whom came Moses, the judges, kings, prophets and finally the Messiah after approximately two-thousand years.

"But when the fullness of the time was come,
God sent forth his Son." (Galatians 4:4)

The Messiah was of the seed of Abraham, of the tribe of Judah, of the house of David and fulfilled all the prophecies pertaining to the first Advent of the "Anointed One". Jesus chose Jewish Apostles to follow him. He also fulfilled the Law completely in His life and ministry. He died a cruel death and rose on the third day. One of the final instructions He gave His disciples was to go to the Jewish and the non-Jewish peoples and teach them.

*"Go ye therefore, and teach all nations,
baptizing them in the name of the Father, and of the Son,
and of the Holy Ghost." (Matthew 28:19)*

The disciples were obedient and therefore the Jewish and the non-Jewish peoples received the Gospel. In the early church an issue unfolded regarding the question, "is God through with the Jew?" Unfortunately, today some ask the same question. The Apostle Paul addresses this most sensitive issue in Romans chapter eleven. Let's look at a few salient points the apostle addresses:

Romans 11

1. **God has not cast away His people (11:1-4)**
   Paul sets forth the argument that he is an Israelite of the seed of Abraham, of the tribe of Benjamin. Simply stated he is a Jew of the highest-water. He reminds his readers that God "foreknew" His people and will not reject them.

2. **A remnant will believe (11:5)**
   The apostle reminds us *"according to the election of grace"* a remnant of Jews will believe that Jesus is the Messiah. This reinforces the idea that the Church should reach out to the Jew with the Gospel.

3. **The Gentile "Great Commission" (11:11-14)**
   Paul plainly states that *"salvation is come unto the Gentiles, for to provoke them to jealousy."* The church is to live in such a fashion that the Jewish community will become jealous over the fact that we believe in their Messiah.

Today, many churches do not have a mission outreach to the Jewish community and yet we read, *"I will bless them that bless thee (the Jew), and curse him that curseth thee (the Jew)." Genesis 12:3*

May churches be challenged to reach the people through whom the Messiah came. Look what the writer of Hebrews states concerning the Messiah:

> *"For verily he took not on him the nature of angels; but he took on him the seed of Abraham" (Hebrews 2:16)*

Below are some practical pointers when witnessing to Jewish people. May God help Christians *"provoke to jealousy"* God's ancient people, *"the seed of Abraham"*, by lovingly reaching out to them with the gospel of Yeshua ha Meshiach, Jesus the Messiah.

Some Practical Pointers when Communicating the Gospel:

1. Love the Lord with all your heart (Deut. 6:5; Mat. 22:37)
2. Love people (Mat. 22:39)
3. Believe the Word of God is Truth (John 17:17)
4. Be patient and sensitive to the needs of those to whom you are speaking (John 4:1-42)
5. Witness in the power of the Holy Spirit depending completely upon God. Don't force the issue (Acts 1:8)
6. Be a good listener (Luke 24:13-35)

7. Share your testimony (Acts 22:1-21)

Listed below is a guide though the Scriptures that communicate the gospel effectively to God's ancient people Israel:

1. *Man is a sinner*
   Ecclesiastes 7:20 – All people are sinners
   Isaiah 64:6 – Our works are filthy in God's sight

2. *Results of sin*
   Isaiah 59:2 – Our relationship with God is severed

3. *God's way of taking away sin*
   Leviticus 17:11 – A blood sacrifice
   Isaiah 53:3-12 – Sacrifice provided by Messiah

4. *When the Messiah is to come*
   Daniel 9:26 – At the end of the 69th week He is to die, just before the destruction of the "sanctuary" of the Temple and the city which occurred in A.D. 70

5. *Salvation is by faith*
   Genesis 15:6 – Abraham believed
   Understanding these few points will help the Christian to effectively witness to their friends and neighbors.

"For I am not ashamed of the gospel of Christ: for it is the power of God unto salvation to every one that believeth; to the Jew first, and also to the Greek." (Romans 1:16)

Chapter 2
David's City

Stone Structures

Walking down the alleyway from my apartment heading towards the main intersection I was struck once again with unique diversity of Jerusalem.

The crescent moon was rising as Shabbat ended and the city began to wake up. I have been to Jerusalem several times now and I attempted to paused and look at it as with new eyes. Everywhere you look you see stone. Stone houses, stone apartments, stone shops, stone high rises. Everywhere is this beautiful, yet foreboding stone. When the sun sets the city looks golden, almost otherworldly.

Soldiers & Secular

Young, old, secular, religious all reside here. Jerusalem is one of the poorest cities in Israel and yet you can find the latest fashion. You see the religious wearing their black or dark clothing. You find soldiers - young men and women, wearing the uniform with M-16's over their shoulder, or a side arm. So young these soldiers look, yet they are ready in a moment to defend their homeland.

Relentless Roulette

Small cars, compact cars everywhere, at times you will see a large SUV. Motor scooters weaving in an out of traffic, busses, these are the busses that terrorists blow up. "Those riding the busses," as one person said, "are playing bus roulette." Arabs, and Jews live side by side. You can feel the tension in the air. Very few people smile. There is difficulty and despair in their eyes. Within the streets you will see a press of people going to and fro.

Saga and Security

These highways and byways echo with history. You walk on stone and behold structures that are centuries old and in some cases millennia old. The Saga continues as your senses are aroused with the smell of meat cooking, with different colored fruits and vegetables in the old city. You hear horns blowing, people talking, some arguing. Everybody watches for anything that doesn't look right, anything suspicious. You hear birds singing, you see walls, fences, steel doors, barbed wire, steel lattice over the windows. Dust everywhere.

Marvel and Mystery

You marvel at the biblical historic mountains with their majestic peaks, trees and stories. The Mount of Olives from the Temple Mount is glorious. The white sepulchers of the religious Jews who wish to be resurrected first when the Messiah descends on the Mount (Zechariah 14) are amassed on the southern slope. The steeple of the Church of Ascension atop of the mount reminds us of Christ's ascension to the Father. On the western face of the mountain you behold the Garden of Gethsemane and the place where Jesus rode triumphantly into Jerusalem. Jerusalem is filled with the mystery and wonder of the story of Christ.

Emotions Engaged

You experience the places where Jesus walked. The Pool of Bethesda where Jesus healed a man. Your heart is moved at the place where He stood before Pilate. You can touch the empty tomb, and gaze upon Calvary. Oh, the religious experience is profound. Every emotion is engaged. One can become almost overwhelmed with all this information coming at you. You tremble and rejoice all at the same time. David walked this area, the prophets came here, and the apostles dwelt here.

Common Courage

And yet, everyday common people live here. They work long hours to eek out a living. Everything is hard here. Nothing is easy. You admire their strength, courage, and tenacity. Many Jews make their "aliyah" (moving to Israel) from other countries not knowing why they come. They just felt they had to relocate. Some come for religious reasons. You will find Christians here, very few however. Jews and Muslims make up most of the construct of Israel.

Overwhelming Occurrences

Every once in a while you will find someone who has, what the Israelis call, "the Messiah syndrome" or "the Jerusalem syndrome," meaning a religious person, Jewish or Christian, will be so overwhelmed that they begin to preach, or blow the ram's horn on the corner or mountain top, or along the wall of the old city.

Ruling and Reigning

Jerusalem has a powerful effect on people. After all, as the rabbis say, it is the "center of the earth." In fact they emphasize it is the "center of the universe." In this they are correct. Jerusalem is where Jesus will rule and reign for a thousand years. He will return to the Mount of Olives and then enter the city. No wonder Jerusalem creates fear and wonder in the hearts of men Psalm 48. Let's look at some facts regarding Jerusalem:

Historically:

1. The first mention of Jerusalem is found in Genesis 14:8 where the city is called Salem. Salem means "peace."

2. Ezekiel mentions that the area was once populated by the Amorites and Hittites (Ezekiel 16:3).

3. Jerusalem is also in the area of Moriah where Abraham bound Isaac (Genesis 22).

4. God gave to David the city, via conquest, from the Jebusites around 1,004 BC, over 3,000 years ago (1 Chronicles 11:4-9).

5. David bought a threshing floor for 50 shekels of silver (2 Samuel 24:24) and built an altar unto the Lord. (same area where Abraham bound Isaac)

6. This threshing floor is where Solomon, David's son, built the Temple (2 Chronicles 3:1).

7. This is the site of the second temple and the temple that Herod embellished in the time of Jesus.

8. Jesus rode into the city as people praised and worshiped Him as Messiah.

9. Jesus was crucified outside Jerusalem's walls.

10. Jesus ascended to the Father from the Mount of Olives overlooking the Temple.

The Future:

1. This will also be the sight of the Tribulation Temple (2 Thessalonians 2:1-4).

2. Jerusalem will be hated by all nations (Zechariah 12:2,3).

3. Jerusalem will be surrounded by armies (Zechariah 14:1,2).

4. Messiah will descend in this area (Zechariah 14:3,4).

5. This is where the Millennial Temple will stand (Ezekiel 40; Zechariah 2,3).

6. God desires Jerusalem (Psalm 132:14).

7. Jerusalem will be the center of Messiah's Kingdom.

8. Jerusalem will be the global capital (Isaiah 2:2-4).

We can begin to understand the beauty, significance and wonder of Jerusalem.

Chapter 3
Being Israeli

The Plane

In London, while waiting on the plane in anticipation of take off, an announcement was made. *"Ladies and gentlemen we will have a slight delay. We are unable to start the engine."* Thirty minutes had gone by. Forty-five minutes. By this time the plane load of mostly Jewish people going home to Israel began to visit and laugh, playing with their children and introducing each other. It was a wonderful sense of community. As Louise and I sat there we also began to chat with some of the folks and have interaction with the others.

There was an incredible sense that we will survive this ordeal. Two hours had passed before the mechanics were able to fix the problem with the engine. Rather than being upset, there was camaraderie. It reminded me of what the early church must have been like. Shoulder to shoulder, back to back, we will stick together and help each other and support one another. Protect the children and watch over the old ones, together we stand, together we fall. Wow! What an experience.

If this was an average plane load of Americans, there would have been anger, frustration and complaining for the loss of time. If this was the average church and something didn't work out just the way was supposed too, there would have been complaining, whining, gossip and division and perhaps a desire to recall the pastor.

The Rabbi

Days after we landed in Israel and settled into our apartment Louise and I, along with some friends, visited a religious Jewish school which was operated by a local rabbi and his small synagogue. They had an outreach to the poor in their community in which they helped with the basic food needs by supplying one meal a day for each member of the families in need. School supplies and some clothing were also provided for those who had school age children. Their school is like a day school teaching and caring for children 2-6 years of age.

The rabbi is a gentle man with a tender heart for those in need within his community. He had shown us where the children were napping. He opened the door and there they were, about a dozen children 3 or 4 years of age sleeping on mats on the floor. They looked like little cherubs from heaven, trusting, safe and sound asleep.

While showing us this sacred place where the children were asleep, this kind rabbi made a profound statement. With a twinkle in his eye he said, *"When I feel discouraged I come here to look at the children. And when I do, my heart finds joy."* In our conversation together we both acknowledged that children are a blessing from God and this is why we find joy in the little ones.

The Bomb

Several days later while traveling through the West Bank we found ourselves in a Jewish settlement visiting a family who experienced what no family should ever experience. Their story goes like this. The family was going on vacation to Kenya, Africa. Many Israelis go there as it is an inexpensive way to go on vacation from Israel. After a long year of working in the mines, the father wanted to bless his family with a long needed vacation. So with tickets in hand they boarded the plane and headed for Kenya. As the plane was descending, and just about to land, terrorists launched a deadly missile. You may recall reading this in the news some time ago. The terrorist's objective was to bring down this Israeli aircraft and kill everyone on board. Fortunately, the missile missed its target. They landed safely.

Later, after surviving the missile attack, the family checks into the hotel. The overdue family vacation had begun. Mom and the three children, two sons (teenagers) and a daughter (9), wanted to go down to the main lobby area and to check things out and look around the area. Dad stayed in the room resting. Little did they know that evil once again was lurking around the corner. A suicide bomber plotted a dishonorable, immoral, base deed. While the mother and three children were in the lobby this demon blew himself up, killing many people in the hotel, including the two teenage sons. Mom was severely wounded and burned. Daughter was burned. After a year of physical therapy mom can walk short distances. Her right leg is completely numb with no feeling whatsoever. Their daughter still has nightmares and is having challenges adjusting to regular life. Dad blames himself for not being there with his family. *"Maybe, I could have saved them from this attack. I should have been there"*, he continually says. He is in therapy for depression and despair. They still mourn the loss of their two boys.

The Gift

Oftentimes when I speak in churches and colleges I address the important subject that, *"life is precious"*. Here in Israel it is not about being Jewish, but rather, being Israeli. Let me explain. Within this tiny country you have Jews from the former Soviet Union, Europe, Africa, India, North America and every corner of the world you can imagine, 6 ½ million people. You have a labyrinth of cultures and religious expression. Everyone, who is able, will go into the military. It is the way of life here. Young people go through the military and once their duty is complete, they travel for year if they can afford to do so. Then off to university.

Life is a precious commodity. It is so fragile here and it is a hard life. Terrorism, the economy, taxes to name just a few. Every moment is a gift. Every life experience and life stage is precious. To be identified as Israeli is very important. To have the Israeli experience is to be immersed in understanding what survival is and the sacrifice necessary to live here. One father from India said it was much easier living in India than Israel. Nevertheless, they are committed to staying in the Land of the Bible as they felt somehow compelled to come to this promise land.

The scripture is replete with passages concerning Jews coming to Israel from all over the world. From the north, south, east and west they will come. They will come and restore Israel in the end times. You can see it in their eyes, hear it in their words and see it in their actions. They are committed to staying and living in the Land God has promised them.

"Pray for the peace of Jerusalem:
they shall prosper that love thee."
~Psalm 122:6

"Inasmuch as ye have done it unto one of the least of these my brethren, ye have done it unto me."
~Matthew 25:40

Chapter 4
A Day In Worship

On Shabbat the streets were pretty empty as religious Jews observe the day of rest. Louise and I walked down the street and you could sense an eerie otherworld feeling in the air. You could hear our steps echo off the stone buildings and paved streets.

Back in Time

We approached the door of the little book store located in the heart of the Orthodox Jewish community in Jerusalem. I pushed on the glass and opened the squeaky door. The lights were off as we meandered through the multitudinous isles and shelves of books to the back room where there were a few others gathering. Walking up a spiraling stairway we found ourselves in a tiny sanctuary made of stone walls above the bookstore. Electric wires hung down from the partially finished ceiling. To the right you could look out an arched shape window overlooking the ancient streets of Jerusalem. Your imagination could take you back millennia and envision you were with first century followers of Jesus of Nazareth.

The padded theater-like chairs were welcoming the worshippers as one-by-one Jewish people came silently, respectfully. (There were a few Gentiles also in attendance). The sanctuary could seat perhaps 50 people. In the front, an altar covered by a prayer shawl was the central focus. You would see a lighted menorah, torah scroll and shofar, Shabbat candles, communion cup and bread.

The songs sung were a blended mix of Israeli melodies of worship, traditional hymns and praise songs (Israeli style). To the left of the altar was a piece of furniture that looked like an armoire which was filled with holy books, bibles, hymnals, prayer and song books. To the right of the altar was the pulpit where the beloved pastor, who was draped with a prayer shawl over his shoulders, led the worship, liturgy, and teaching/preaching of the Scripture. All the service was spoken in Hebrew with an English translator (the pastor's wife) seated in a row for those needing translation.

The Lord's Table

Towards the end of the worship service, believers in Jesus, and those who were scripturally baptized (by immersion) were encouraged to observe communion. The people with great reverence began to form a line. The pastor took the bread and gave it to each worshipper standing in the line. He would give a brief explanation stating the bread represented the body of Messiah and then bless each person with a pastoral blessing. He would then pray and we all partook of the bread together. He would do the same thing with the wine explaining this represents the blood of our Lord. This holy man would look deep into each person's eyes, making this ancient religious rite very personal, with a big smile, and at times with tears, and then bless each congregant with a little prayer. Louise and I were moved deeply by this experience. However, there was something even more surprising.

A Different Blessing

Two of the people standing in line solemnly bowed as the pastor gently and lovingly, raising his hand touched them on top of their heads, and gave them a blessing that was a little different from the other blessings. As he raised his right hand you could see on his prayer shawl the fringes on the corners and sides swinging loosely in the air. He did not give them bread, nor the wine. It was quite a moment to see the tears and genuine expression of Christ's love. After communion the congregation began to slowly walk toward their seats, with arms around each other with authentic love for one another. At the conclusion of the service, the people stood and the pastor covered his head and shoulders with the prayer shawl giving the final benediction.

After the worship service I asked the pastor, "What did you do to those two who did not receive the bread and wine?" He stated with great love, "You see my brother, these two do not yet know the Lord. They simply come down to receive a blessing from the man of God."

What a lesson! These two people came because they knew this is where people of God meet. These two precious individuals came forward to be blessed by the man of God. They saw something in the congregation and in the man of God that was profoundly different. They came enough to know they were not yet believers, and yet they felt loved and welcomed within the community of those who believe in Jesus. There was no one within this tiny community of saints who rejected these two who did not know the Lord.

Salt & Light

This pastor is teaching God's people well by word and deed. He was showing them by example how to be salt and light bringing hope to a world in desperate need of the Savior. May we who claim to be followers of Christ do the same and be a blessing to our neighbors and surrounding communities. Together, let's reach out our hands in the name of Jesus our Lord and bless the people God puts in our lives! What would Jesus do? Let us go and do likewise.

Your prayers and financial support for Louise and me enable us to feed thousands within Israel and the Middle East. Your support also allows us to be an encouragement to this beloved pastor and his wife as well as other Christian leaders in the Middle East. May God bless you, as you bless Abraham's seed through Israel Today Ministries!

Chapter 5
Is It Safe There?

The Temple Mount

It is sobering to be reminded of the disdain toward Westerners in the Middle East, specifically within the Muslim Arab construct. Recently, while on the Temple Mount you could feel the tension and mistrust as Palestinian security watched us on every turn with their walkie talkies whispering communications to someone as to the direction of our trek.

Leaving the Temple Mount we could see, and feel the stares of contempt and gestures of cursing us from Muslim fundamentalists sitting near their famous Mosque. On the one hand, it was wonderful to be up on the mount to see where the Temple stood and to stand in the location of the Holy of Holies. It was moving from the Temple site to see the Mount of Olives nearby, the place where Jesus will descend, and to realize that He will rule and reign from this very spot on the Temple Mount. And yet, on the other hand, it was good to disengage from being in the place where the Dome of the Rock and the El Aqsa Mosque now stand.

The Driver

Then there was the Arab taxi driver who took us to the Mount of Olives showing us a new view of the old city. Yes it was a nice view, however getting there was suspicious as he took us down a narrow dirt and rocky pass. A white van came out of no where and slowly traveled passed us and turned around facing us, parking about thirty yards down the way.

At first we wondered if this was an attempt to kidnap or to harm us, but then, we were tired, jet lagged and our minds were simply running away with us.

The driver wanted to show us his family place of business and have a cup of tea together. I politely said no. He became angry and verbally derided Americans who "spend millions of dollars in Israel and let the Palestinians starve."

We then came to our final destination. He wanted to charge us some outrageous fee. I refused to pay his suggested fee. We haggled and then came to an agreement. Another Arab who was nearby saw and heard the exchange and apologized for that driver's behavior. He said that the driver does not represent the Arab community. He said, "all we want to do is live in peace."

A Reminder

Now these are unusual circumstances indeed. This is not an anti-Arab article. There are Arab families who are kind and only desire to live in peace. There are Arab families who believe in and love Jesus. I know many of these kind and loving families and they tell me, "please tell those in America that the Islamic militants do not represent us."

For me, when I enter a Jewish community, or the Jewish quarter in the old city, I feel at ease. You will see families walking together, for the most part shop keepers are friendly and you sense a different spirit. Security is everywhere.

Do You Feel Safe?

Often I am asked to you feel safe in Israel? My answer is, "Yes!" I would never bring my wife or loved ones to a place that was not safe. Is there danger? "Of course." However, there is danger walking the streets of San Diego. You simply have to be aware of your location and have someone with you who knows where it is safe. Certain areas you avoid, just like in any city or country.

What's Going On?

The children of Abraham are odds with each other. This comes to no surprise to the student of the Bible. Genesis 16 tells us that Abraham's seed will have struggles with each other. This is why we pray, "Thy kingdom come, Thy will be done, on earth as it is in heaven." You see, there will be no peace until the Prince of Peace comes and establishes His kingdom on earth. When we "pray for the peace of Jerusalem" (Psalm 122:6) we are praying, "Thy Kingdom come" (Matthew 6:10).

Our Goal

We will continue to go to Israel. In fact, Louise and I will ultimately be staying months at a time there as God provides the finances. One day there will be peace. Until then, Israel needs our help and encouragement. The Scriptures tell us that the nations will turn against Israel. Even today, there is a growing anti- Semitism throughout the world. Israel will be blamed for the wows of the world.

We must stand with God's ancient people Israel and pray for peace and aid her in this time of need.

Lessons Learned

There are good Jews. There are bad Jews. There are good Arabs. There are bad Arabs. As Christians we have the privilege of presenting to the world the message of God's redeeming grace through Jesus Christ our Lord.

It's not so much what we say, but what we do. It's not about our creeds, though obviously important, it's not about our beautiful edifices, however impressive, it's not about our talk or outward appearance, as much as it is what we do. Jewish people will not hear your words, until they hear your life. In fact, I believe, most people are like that.

The Jewish Way

The religious Jews have a word that describes walking the walk. Halakha, or *the Jewish way* . This is what Paul was referring to:

"We should walk in newness of life" (Rom. 6:4)
"We walk by faith" (2 Cor. 5:7)
"Walk worthy" (Eph. 4:1)

When rabbi Sha'ul (Paul) was talking about "walking" he was referring to halakha. Halakha simply means, "the way on which one goes." Basically, this is about behavior or a practical manifestation of our beliefs and doctrine. James, the brother of our Lord and first pastor of the first church said it this way, "Be doers of the word" & "I will show you my faith by my works" (James 1:22; 2:18).

Fleshing out what we say we believe, speaks louder than anything we say. Jesus said that we are to love God with all our heart and then to love each other. And by this all will know that we are genuine disciples, or followers of Messiah (Mark 12:29-31; John 13:34,35).

Disappearing

One of the principles of halakha is that of having a mark of distinction. The way on which a Christian should go is to emulate Jesus. For religious Jews it is to emulate Torah (first five books of Moses).

To compromise and assimilate into the world, a religious Jew fears that the mark of distinction, of being an observant Jew, would be lost. In other words if a Jew disregards the importance of halakha, Judaism may disappear.

In the same vein, if Christians begin to assimilate into the world, and loose their identity, their mark of distinction and testimony of truth may disappear or become powerless.

Finally

In a world where there is hatred, despair, fear and a lack of hope may believers in Jesus stay the course. May we keep our distinctive Christian character and not assimilate into the world and loose our identity. May we walk the walk in such a way that the world will know we follow Jesus.

Jewish people, now more than ever, are open to message of Messiah Yeshua. Let us be a faithful witness to Israel and not fail our commission to "the Jew first".

Pray for the peace of Jerusalem! The days that are ahead may be difficult. Now is the time to act and to walk "the way on which one goes."

Your good deeds and prayers are part of your halakha.

God will bless those who bless Israel. It is a promise (Genesis 12:3).

Until He comes, we are together under His wings (Psalm 91).

Chapter 6
Prophecy Regarding Israel

In these days of growing turmoil in the world, with the nation of Israel being in the center of world concern, the subject of prophecy can be greatly used in sharing your faith. When discussing prophecy consider sharing the following:

1. God chose Israel as a nation (Psalm 135:4)

2. God loves Israel (Deuteronomy 7:6-8)

3. God's love for Israel is eternal (Jeremiah 31:3)

4. Israel was chose to be a witness for God (Deuteronomy 6:4; 33:26-29)

5. Israel was chosen to receive and preserve God's revelation of Himself (Romans 3:1,2)

6. Through Israel would come the Messiah (Isaiah 7:14)

7. Israel will be preserved (Jeremiah 31:35,36)

8. God will bless those who bless Israel and curse those who curse Israel (Genesis 12:1-3)

9. That all the families of the earth will be blessed because the Messiah will come through Israel (Genesis 12:1-3)

10. God promised Israel a gift of land (Genesis 17:8)

11. That Israel will experience dispersion:
    a. Into Egypt (Genesis 15:13,14)
    b. Into Babylon (Jeremiah 25:11,12)
    c. Into the World (Deuteronomy 28:62-68)

12. That Israel will be restored in the last days:
    a. In unbelief (Ezekiel 37:8,11)
    b. In believing that Jesus is the Messiah (Ezekiel 37:14; Zechariah 12:10; 14:16)
    c. Never to uprooted again (Amos 9:11-15)